HELP! MY DOG IS A DEVIL WITH OTHER DOGS

The proactive approach to help your reactive dog

Tim Jackson

Copyright © 2020 by Tim Jackson

Published by WriterMotive
www.writermotive.com

Contents

Praise for our one to one behaviour course...5

Introduction 7

Chapter One: My dog is trying to take over the household! 11

Chapter Two: Why your dog turns into the devil incarnate 16

Chapter Three: Understanding your dog's language................................. 24

Chapter Four: Helping them deal with the stresses life can throw at us 33

Chapter Five: 'Look at me' 44

Chapter Six: Turn Around 52

Chapter Seven: It's ok, my dog's friendly 57

Chapter Eight: Your goal for success 61

Bonuses.. 65

About the Author.. 66

Acknowledgements 68

Praise for our one to one behaviour course

What some of our clients have to say about our one to one behaviour course

"Our three-year-old west highland terrier wasn't responding well to our new shih tzu puppy. We'd expected jealousy etc, but he was really fearful and became aggressive, withdrawn and generally seemed depressed. He'd stopped playing with us, and we were getting to the point of returning our puppy.

Tim came out and spent some time with us and our westie… of course, it was us that got the training lol! Tim was brilliant, gave an honest assessment of our situation and changes we could make immediately as well as training exercises we could do with the dogs.
After perseverance and practice, we now have 2 happy dogs and the confidence to continue with the work. I can definitely recommend Tim. Thanks so much for a happier life."
Vicki Kenyon

"I have a one-year-old red cocker and was having a lot of problems with his behaviour – my fault as I totally spoilt him from day one. Tim was recommended by my dog groomer. I rang and booked a telephone consultation. I felt at ease as soon as I spoke to him. He was so lovely and made me feel positive from the start.
He came out for a visit, and I loved his modern methods of training. After our initial consultation, Tim appointed one of his trainers, Lauren, to continue with the course. I was a little apprehensive as I hadn't met her and she hadn't met our dog.
One week later, Lauren came for our first training appointment. She was absolutely fantastic, very knowledgeable about our situation and what we needed to achieve.
The training methods set out by Tim were great, I felt very comfortable with Lauren, and she definitely knew what she was doing.
We got out of the programme everything we needed. It's up to us now to keep putting in the work we learnt.
After the first lesson, we saw a huge improvement in our dog's behaviour.

I would definitely recommend Tim, Lauren and Pets2impress."
Sara White

"We bought two puppies and found it extremely difficult to do anything with them; we needed help.
We got with Tim at Pets2impress, who came and did an assessment. He informed us that they had fear-based aggression towards other dogs, and he put our minds at ease knowing that there was something we could do to help them.
We then had lessons with Lauren, who taught me exactly what to do, which gave me the confidence to give them the help and training they needed.
Without Tim and Lauren's help, I could not have coped. I can't recommend them enough."
Mr and Mrs Selby

"My partner and I adopted a dog from Europe. All was well until 3 months later when he started to show signs of aggression towards other dogs and men.
We contacted Tim for an assessment and booked on for training. We did everything Tim suggested, and now our dog can be around other dogs (even daycare) and people.
We now have learnt the tools and techniques needed to recognise when our dog is in a situation he is not comfortable with and able to use the training commands to get him out of it which means no more aggression! Thank you Tim"
Mr S Scott

Introduction

In the United Kingdom, it is estimated that 12 million households have pets, with 25% of those households having a dog. Out of that 25%, 42% of owners report their dog as being aggressive.

This is a huge number which is why I tell all owners that have a reactive dog, **YOU ARE NOT ALONE.**

So many owners believe they have failed and so many owners struggle to understand why their dog reacts like this.

I was one of those owners. Let me tell you about my old dog, Lady, who was a beautiful German Shepherd. Lady grew up with other dogs; she used to love going to the beach and playing with other dogs… don't get me wrong she had a number of issues shall we say (I could write a whole book on Lady!) but one thing was for sure she loved interacting and socialising with other dogs.

As she started to get older, if I remember correctly, she was about 6/7 years old, and we were out on a walk at the beach. She was playing with one of her canine friends, Sasha, who she had played with on numerous occasions. It was very common for these two to play rough and chase one another. This one particular day something out of the ordinary happened, after a few minutes of normal play, Lady yelped and got into a scuffle with Sasha. At the time, I presumed Sasha must have nipped her during play and thought nothing more of it.

A few days later a similar incident between Lady and another dog occurred, and as the weeks passed, she was starting to do it to more and more dogs, and she got to a stage where she was wanting to chase off other dogs that were approaching her. Naturally, I was thrown and at the time I thought could it be due to that one negative association with Sasha? After all, it can sometimes only take one negative association.

As a veterinary nurse and knowing the type of breed Lady was, I decided to take her to the vets to rule out anything medical. She had an x-ray, and it turned out she had arthritis. She was put on medication to help with the pain and inflammation, and after some training and positive reinforcement, I got her to a stage where she started to want to interact with her canine friends again.

It was a frustrating time though, especially with how out of the blue, it all came. I found it incredibly difficult to walk Lady who was lunging, barking and often trying to attack other dogs.

As a dog owner, we have a huge responsibility, and that doesn't just involve making sure our dog is fit and well and providing them with what they need. We also have a responsibility for their actions as well.

I did not want to have to live a life of waking up at 4:30am to take Lady for a walk to avoid other dogs and their owners. I enjoyed my walks with Lady, and I enjoyed being out with her. I am a family man, and I enjoy being out during the day with the family, which included Lady. To have a reactive dog was not an option I was prepared to live with.

Unfortunately, that responsibility is too much for some owners; after all, it is difficult to deal with this behaviour problem. Throughout the country, there are at a lot of dogs that end up in shelters due to their problematic behaviours towards other dogs; this is certainly something I found when I worked for Dogs Trust. Some owners find it incredibly difficult and they feel they have exhausted all options and the reality of owning a dog like this proves to be too much so rehoming or sending the dog to an animal shelter is sometimes the easiest option.

Sadly so many dogs in shelter get euthanised, and although in a lot of cases this is the last resort, it breaks my heart as sometimes, a little bit of hard work and regular training will help to correct this problematic behaviour.

Dogs can be reactive for a number of reasons; in Lady's case, it was pain-related. This book will help you understand why your dog is reactive towards other dogs, and it will give you a practical guide on how to correct this problematic behaviour focusing only on positive based methods of training.

This book was created to try and prevent dogs from ending up in a shelter and to help make your walks enjoyable again by giving a simple step by step guide on what you need to do to recondition your dog's behaviour and build up a positive association around other dogs. The book is designed for anyone that has a reactive dog and for those that feel they have 'tried everything else.'

I do not believe in choke chains, spray collars, shock collars or any form of negative based methods of training so if that is what you are looking for, I suggest you look elsewhere. A lot of the time a reactive dog is already in a negative situation when around other dogs. Using negative based methods of training will add further negative arousal and will never correct the problem; in fact, there is a good chance it will make the problem worse.

There is no point in reading this book and then putting in on the shelf and thinking 'oh that was a good read'. You need to put in the work and understand that any form of behaviour modification can take a lot of time and patience.

Once you have read this book, you will understand how to correct this behaviour in your dog, but firstly, we need to understand why our dog is reacting the way he is.

Chapter One

My dog is trying to take over the household!

I am guessing everyone reading this book is in the same position? Stressed walks? Avoiding all other dogs? Walking your dog at stupid times of the day just so that you do not bump into any other dogs?

The number of people I speak to on a daily basis that get up at 4am just so they can walk their dog and avoid coming into contact with other dogs is growing. It's honestly crazy, I couldn't imagine living my life like that (I need my beauty sleep), but soon with the help of this book that will be unnecessary.

Correct me if I am wrong, but that's not why we got a dog right? Dogs don't have to cause us stress or upset and likewise, dogs should not have to feel stressed or upset. They are only on this earth for a short amount of time surely, we owe it to the dog that we love, the dog that we class as part of our family to ensure that they are happy.

Before you can stop your dog from lunging, barking, snarling or just generally acting problematically around other dogs, there is one very important question you need to ask yourself and that question is WHY?

In order to correct problematic behaviour, you firstly need to understand WHY your dog is reacting the way he is, only then can you truly do something about it and that is exactly what I will begin to cover in this chapter.

As humans we are able to explain to one another the emotions we are feeling (sometimes maybe we do not handle it as well as we could, i.e. we shout or we slam doors) unfortunately dogs do not have that luxury which is one of the reasons I think so many owners get stressed and frustrated when it comes to owning a reactive dog.

Before we look at the main reasons why your dog is reacting the way he is around other dogs I am going to start by telling you one of the reasons your dog is NOT reacting the way he is.

As a canine behaviourist, I give owners the option to book a free telephone consultation so that we can discuss the issues the owner is experiencing with their dog whether it be behavioural or training but there is one thing I hear at least three times a day; "my dog is being dominant!"

The dominance theory

The word dominance is a word I very rarely use, and when I hear someone say it, I know I have my work cut out as sadly so many people believe their dogs are trying to dominate them, trying to take over the house, trying to be dominant around other dogs.

If you look at the definition of the word 'dominant' in the Collins Dictionary, this is what it says

"Someone or something that is **dominant** is more powerful, successful, influential, or noticeable than other people or things."

https://www.collinsdictionary.com/dictionary/english/dominant

Answer me this! Why on earth would your dog want to be more powerful or successful than you? Correct me if I am wrong but do you feed your dog? Do you walk your dog? Do you buy your dog new toys, treats? If your dog does any of the above, then please give me a call, I would love to hear about it!

Why would a dog want to dominate you when you provide everything for them? When you start to think of it like that it now seems a bit silly, doesn't it? (I can hear you saying "Yes Tim"). The issue with the dominance theory is so many owners believe that their dog is trying to achieve higher social 'status'; therefore, to correct this, the owner needs to establish 'dominance' over the dog and implement it as part of their training plan…. WRONG!

I can all but guarantee that implementing the dominance theory will end up resulting in one thing… you getting bitten… dog gets put to sleep! I hate to be so black and white, but I see and hear this day in, day out.

I will always remember a dog I went to see a lovely little spaniel called Bluey. From the history given by the owners, Bluey was displaying aggression around certain toys, chews and he hated going in the car (he only went in the car to go to the groomers) and they sought the help from a "trainer" who advised that they must show Bluey who is boss! The so-called "trainer" visited the owner's house for an appointment and apparently after speaking to the owner Bluey growled at the trainer and then hid behind the sofa.

The Trainer then grabbed Bluey out of the sofa by the scruff of the neck (sounds like a lovely person right) and explained to the owner that this behaviour was not acceptable and that he needed to show Bluey who was in charge.

The trainer shouted, and Bluey, at this point, wet himself purely out of fear. The trainer advised the owner to implement a training programme which followed the dominance style methods of training and guess what happened... the owner got bit time and time again and the dog lost all trust and confidence in her, and she lost all trust and confidence in her dog.

She finally got in touch with me to which I was appalled by the training tips (if you can call them that) that she had been advised to implement and it took a very long time, and lots of hard work before Bluey started to trust his owner again with the help from someone who actually knew what they were talking about and someone that used up to date proven methods of training (positive based methods of training).

Imagine if our lives were lived in a way where we tried to dominate our partners (I wouldn't stand a chance with my wife!), that is not what a relationship is built on. A relationship is built on trust and love.

I will always remember watching Coronation Street (That's right, I'm a soap man) back in 2012 with the domestic violence storyline between Tyrone Dobbs and Kirsty Soames. I personally found it very difficult to watch, but unfortunately, we do live in a world where this happens.

The vulnerability and fear displayed by Alan Halsall, who plays the character Tyrone, was incredible. The way this storyline was delivered helped a lot of people come forward and speak out. That is something we have the luxury of, a voice! Unfortunately, dogs don't have a voice and spend a lot of their life in fear as owners attempt to inflict the dominance theory.

No dog should have to live a life of fear!

So where did the dominance theory come from and why do so many people still use it?

Back in the 1970s, there was a study carried out on wolves in captivity. Now it is important to remember that these wolves were not related and they were all placed into one enclosure and observed for behaviour. The evidence gathered showed that these wolves fought over resources such as food, sleeping areas and mates and the studies suggested that there was a hierarchy system in place with the 'alpha' (the leader) having first dibs at everything.

Therefore they were branded as a dominant species, and because dogs were believed to have descended from wolves, then they too were branded as a dominant species that were trying to take over our households and be the 'Alpha' of the pack... what a load of dog poo!

How many of you watch Big Brother? Back in the day, when I had very little to do (you know before marriage, before children when you seem to have more time to yourself), I used to enjoy watching Big Brother but what happened? What made it good TV? A bunch of strangers were placed in this one house and viewed by millions of people but let's be honest what kept us gripped the most? The arguments, the bitchy comments, the moaning! Strip that all back and what were the arguments, the bitchy comments and the moaning all over... Resources!!

The creators of Big Brother knew this, which is why limited supplies of things were placed in the house to encourage arguments and why because that makes good Television! If you look at this scenario of the Big Brother house then surely it makes sense as to why these unrelated wolves in captivity also displayed the behaviours that they did...not because they were dominant but because they were stressed, they were frustrated!

Very recently, with thanks to modern technologies we are now able to get up close to wolves in the wild (I love a bit of David Attenborough!), and there is no evidence to suggest that wolves are a dominant species they live very similar to the way we do as a family and they work together as a family to ensure the survival of the pack.

I am sure you have heard 'trainers' mention in the past about how you need to establish the alpha role within your household if you want to have a better-behaved dog. Let us have a look at some of the methods of training that these 'trainers' advise people to implement and you let me know your thoughts!

- Pin your dog down to the floor if he is 'misbehaving' and hold him there until he is calm
- Eat before your dog
- Leave a room before your dog
- Be more assertive with your dog
- Take your dogs food away as they are eating, so he knows 'you are the boss.'

You must agree this is ridiculous! The problem with the dominance theory (apart from it being a huge pile of dog poop) is it causes stress for your dog and in a lot of cases can cause fear. Please correct me if I am wrong, but this is not why we got a dog; we got a dog to be apart of the family and to be loved. I do appreciate at times when you are at the end of your tether you want results and you want results now, but I hate to break it to you that's not how it works with dog training. Dog training requires time, patience and consistency.

So before we move on to WHY our dog is reacting the way he is, I want you to digest the dominance theory. You may have used it in the past, you may be using it now. BUT as the crazy monkey from The Lion King once said, "it's in the past it doesn't matter!" it's what we do from now that really counts.

In order to move forward, we need to stop using old-style methods of training and focus on positive based methods of training as these methods have been proven time and time again to work.

So now that is out the way, and you are ready to move forward with your dog and step into the 21st century. Let us have a look at some of the reasons why your dog is reacting the way he does towards other dogs.

Chapter Two

Why your dog turns into the devil incarnate

I find as an owner myself, it is important to understand why a dog reacts the way he does because if you understand why then it puts you at a better advantage of trying to correct the problem. So what makes your dog appear to be the devil in carnet when he comes across another dog?

Throughout this chapter, we will be looking at a number of reasons why your dog reacts the way he does. Let's start by looking at one of the most common reasons.

Inadequate socialisation

I am sure you have heard the term socialisation at some point during your time as a dog owner. Socialisation is a very important aspect of owning a dog but one that so many let slip by. A well-socialised puppy will grow up to be confident, more stable and have better coping skills as he grows up.

The key socialisation window for a puppy is between 8-14 weeks old, and although I appreciate a big chunk of that time is during the vaccination period when dogs need to be kept off the ground outside, there are ways around that. There is nothing stopping you from taking your puppy out in your arms or arranging friends and family dogs to come by and visit (providing they are fully vaccinated of course).

I find a lot of owners these days are in fact scared of other dogs so they keep their dog away from other dogs as they fear something may go wrong or they worry that their dog may get hurt. If you live your life on the what-if factor you will never get anywhere and neither will your dog. I understand that this little ball of fluff is your 'baby' but you are doing him no favours by stopping him from being a dog.

A lack of socialisation at an early age can lead to a dog that is fearful of people, dogs, experiences and new places. It is important to remember that early life experiences or should I say a lack of experiences can shape a dog's behaviour.

A negative experience

It is not uncommon for a dog who has been adequately socialised and has enjoyed in the past playing with other dogs to suddenly become reactive, especially if he has had a negative experience with another dog.

Imagine this, you are walking your dog, enjoying the surroundings and being out with your dog and then all of a sudden, a dog comes out of nowhere and sinks his teeth into your dog. How are you going to feel? Maybe this has already happened to you?

Chances are we would be shook up, but what impact has that left on the dog? Sometimes due to this one negative experience, a dog can develop fear, and when a dog is frightened or placed in a situation they feel they cannot escape, emotions take over and like all mammals, they will either choose to fight or flight.

Sometimes a one-off incident can easily be turned around, but if he gets attacked again by another dog, this dog is going to start seeing all other dogs as a potential threat.

Unfortunately, dogs most at risk of being attacked are your brachycephalic breeds (short-faced dogs) and black dogs. The reason for this is simply because other dogs find it difficult to read their body language due to their wrinkles, prominent eyes and stiff stance. Dogs, therefore, assume that they are displaying threatening behaviours and attack.

Imagine this, every time you go to the corner shop, you get punched, just for stepping through the door. Would you keep going? Unless you are built like Arnold Schwarzenegger and can give as good as you get, chances are you will not go back to that shop and why? Because you are scared. Negative experiences can and do happen all of the time and just like dogs we learn from these experiences and learn to act appropriately i.e., in this case, we avoid the corner shop because we can, dogs do not always get that luxury.

Medical

I'll always remember when my wife was in labour, she said things to me, did things to me that I know she didn't really mean (I'll not share them with you as the pain is still there) but that's what pain can do to a person. It is exactly the same with dogs!

There was once a dog called Honey, who was an adorable American Bulldog that I had the pleasure of working with. Honey had been a client of Pets2impress for a couple of years and was a very sociable and friendly dog. One day her owner got in touch with me and explained there had been an 'incident' on her walk.

Every evening Honey would go out for a walk with her owner, and they would meet up with Honey's owners' friends and their dogs. Honey always enjoyed being off lead and playing with her friends. Her owner advised that throughout the day, she did not seem to be herself but explained she was still eating and drinking. She said she just appeared to be quieter than normal.

She was keen to go for her walk and happy to greet her friends, however on this occasion Honey was bounding around with her friend, which was a normal occurrence and during a rough and tumble she yelped and bit her friend. The owner was naturally horrified as this was completely out of character for Honey, so she put her back on the lead and then came back home. Once home she called me for advice.

As this was out of character for Honey, I advised a visit to the veterinary practice to rule out any medical issues. The owner took Honey to the vets, and it turned out she had an ear infection.

Pain was the cause of this reaction as Honey was one minute happily playing with her friend and then all of a sudden OUCH Honey got a pain and redirected her aggression onto the next moving thing, and that, unfortunately, was her canine friend.

Honey was given antibiotics and drops for her ear infection, and luckily there were no further concerns with her behaviour around other dogs however as mentioned in the introduction Lady displayed reactivity to-

Tim Jackson

wards dogs, and it took a little while (and some positive based methods of training) before she was happy to interact with other dogs again.

The dog gets a positive response.

Whatever is causing the dog to react the way he does, we have to bear in mind that his behaviour nine times out of ten is getting him a positive response because the problem goes away.

Imagine this, you are walking down the street with your dog, and you see ahead of you, another owner and their dog are approaching. Once the dog clocks the other dog, he begins to react, and this gets worse as the dog gets closer. But once the dog goes past and is out of sight your dog stops reacting and WHY? This is because his behaviour got him the positive response, he hoped for i.e. the other dog went away.

This is why you have to think dog when it comes to understanding a behavioural problem because as humans we know and understand that we are walking one way, the other dog owner and their dog are walking the opposite way. Dog's don't think like that, they see an immediate threat that they must react to in order to help get their stress levels back to a normal level. Once that threat goes, they no longer need to react. Simple when you look at it like that!

Humans, us, YOU

It is true, unfortunately we too have a massive part to play in the way our dog reacts around other dogs.

Do you tell your dog off? Do you shorten the lead as you approach another dog? Do you pick your dog up? All of these are big no-no's.

Let's talk about shortening the lead, a classic error made by so many. This is how it goes, your dog is on his lead, sniffing around, and then you spot a dog in the distance. Your gut reaction is to shorten the lead or reel him in if he on an extendable lead (don't get me started on extendable leads, that's a different book altogether).

You no doubt at this stage tense up and make sure to have a good firm grip on that lead whilst repeatedly swearing to yourself inside your head…sound familiar? Believe it or not, I would say 99% of owners with reactive dogs behave like this, but what is it telling our dog? Dogs are incredible little animals, and they can read our body language far better than we can read theirs.

The way we react can reinforce a dog's unwanted behaviour around other dogs. Basically, as we start to tighten the lead, tense up etc. the dog starts to look around, unsure why his human is reacting the way he is and then what does he see? The other dog and because his human is reacting the way he is, then there must be something to be worried about right?

When we see another dog, we have a few choices 1. We turn and run away 2. We take our dog to an area away from the path and wait for the other dog to pass whilst constantly saying Noooo No NO 3. We are brave and walk past, keeping the dog as tight to us as possible.

Let's look at number 3 and see why this could be making our dog's behaviour worse.

The next time you are out and about, and you see some dogs playing, watch how they meet. Dogs naturally will approach another dog at an angle, sometimes that angle will be bigger in some dogs than in others but however big or small there is a reason they do this. This is classed as a calming signal, and if that dog approaching on an angle were to speak Geordie he would say something like "Alreet mate, divvent worry I just wanna be ya mate like."

It is very unusual for a dog to greet head to head and greeting head to head normally results in direct eye contact which can be seen as threatening behaviour from the dog he is trying to be friends with. The reason I'm telling you this is because as owners when we shorten the lead, inadvertently, we force the dog to approach the other dog head to head which in turn can be causing our dog to be reactive towards other dogs when on the lead!

So many people are choosing to get small fluffy dogs these days, which is fine, they make great little dogs; however, they very rarely get to act like dogs because their owners are too protective. Another dog comes running over to investigate and say hi, and what is your first reaction? You pick the dog up... oh look he's invisible now!

I completely understand why you do this, you want to protect your wee one, after all, there are so many horror stories posted on social media about dogs getting attacked by other dogs etc. etc. Let me say something very important… DO NOT LIVE YOUR LIFE ON THE WHAT-IF. I could step outside tomorrow and be hit by a bus, but I'm not going to lie awake all night worrying because it's all hypothetical.

If you pick your dog up, do you think the other dog will just think oh I'll just go now, this little dog does not want to say hello. NO, he is going to be wondering why all of a sudden that wee dog is now all the way up there and what is he going to do? Jump up to find out more; after all, dogs are quite curious little things and believe it or not your dog is not invisible when in your arms.

I'll always remember this one time I was in the park, and I heard a number of screams. I thought someone was being murdered, but no it was a lady being jumped upon by two dogs, who by the way were not showing any signs of 'aggression' they were more interested in saying hello to this little cockerpoo who was being cuddled tightly into the owner's arms. The owner was hysterical, all because she was scared by these two dogs. Going back to what I said previously, dogs are very good at reading our body language, and if we do not give them the chance to socialise and make new friends, then we are going to have problems.

We are responsible for a lot of our dog's bad habits, and unfortunately, in a lot of situations, we actually reinforce a dog's problem by the way we react. We tend to do things such as scream and shout at the dog to 'behave' which in turn adds further negative arousal to an already negative situation.

I think one of the main issues us humans have is we are absolutely hopeless at reading dog's body language which in turn means we miss warning signals and before we know it, it's too late. Don't worry, we will be discussing body language in the next chapter.

I wonder if dog's lived separate to humans whether there would be as many issues that we see today… I'm guessing not.

"He just needs to be around other dogs"

Another classic line I hear from owners. In the past, I have had people contact me and ask if they can bring their dog to our socialisation classes or training classes because their dog does not like other dogs, and they think if their dog gets the opportunity to be around other dogs, then life will be sweet again. I am afraid it doesn't work like this. We have to presume that most cases of dog-dog aggression are down to fear, so I want you to imagine being put in a room with something you are absolutely terrified of.

For me, that would be spiders or anything that moves too fast, so the thought of being in a room with lots of creepy crawlies makes my skin itch. Do you think though if I was locked in a room with these creepy crawlies that my fear would suddenly disappear? Of course, it wouldn't I would be even more scared, and the next time I see just one creepy crawly I am going to remember the fear I experienced when I was put in the room with hundreds of them which in turn will make my fear worse.

Have you ever seen any of the celebrities on I'm a celebrity get me out of here that complete one of the bushtucker trials? They may collect all of the stars, but let's be honest the fear they had before the trial has not gone away just because they have been put in an underground box filled with spiders, rats, snakes etc.

The same happens with dogs and although I am sure you have your dog's best interests at heart trust me when I say this is a big fat NO NO. There are better ways to correct this issue which we will be talking about soon.

The overexcited dog

Now I can speak from experience with this one because my dog, Buddy, who is an excitable little whippet who thinks everyone should be his friend, used to get very excited around other dogs. Even those that didn't want to be his friend, he would not give up. I guess Mr Buddy is a bit like me, persistent and doesn't give up!

Some dogs are naturally very sociable and just enjoy the company of other canine friends or in Buddy's case, he must chase everything. This can prove to be difficult though when you are trying to walk your dog, and they are rearing up, barking, pulling all because they want to say hello. Although your dog isn't behaving 'aggressively' (I hate that word!), he is still behaving problematically and still causing you embarrassment and let's be honest us humans do not like to be embarrassed and appear to not be in control of our dog.

So what to do you if your dog gets overly excited when walking past other dogs? Do you say "He just wants to play"? (CLASSIC LINE), do you get annoyed and pull him away? or do you smile and wait until the distraction is out of sight and tell your dog off? Let's be honest dogs totally understand the emotion of embarrassment, right? Erm nope!

Some dogs get such a positive vibe from being around other dogs and playing and rightfully so, they should get the chance to play and socialise, and a lot of the time this over-excitement is seen due to the fact the dog is just so eager to go and say hello but being on the lead he is restricted from doing so.

I'm a great believer though that when you have your dog out for a walk, you need to be in control, and you need to make yourself the best distraction, and that involves having fun with your dog, playing games, scent work, training, natural agility. These are some of the activities we do with our daycare dogs that go on their adventure walks throughout the day because it helps keep your dog's focus on you. You too can make your dog's walk a fun adventure.

Poor Mr Buddy had to be restricted to lead exercise when he was younger as he broke his leg and he found it incredibly difficult and frustrating not being able to play and run as whippets should do. He would bark, rear up, stand like a meerkat and typically do anything he could just to say "hello". Naturally, this was not good for a dog recovering from surgery, so I had to do something to correct it or should I say recondition his unwanted behaviours (more on that in a later chapter).

There are so many reasons that cause a dog to be reactive or act problematically on the lead, and now we know WHY we now need to know WHAT we can do to correct it. Therefore we must start by being able to read our dog's body language and be able to understand what they are trying to communicate to us.

Chapter Three

Understanding your dog's language

"My dog's wagging his tail but yet still trying to bite!" This is something I hear time and time again. Every time I hear it, I want to bang my head off the wall because to me it shows the lack of understanding us humans have when it comes to communicating with our dog.

People are forever saying to me that they wish their dog spoke English so that they knew what they wanted and how to help them, but in fact, dogs are great at communicating, it is us humans that aren't so good at it.

Believe it or not, our dogs can probably understand us more than we can understand them. Dogs are able to read your body language and tone of voice. They will always gaze slightly to the right side of your face - as, although you may not realise it, a human's face reacts on the right before it reacts on the left. They are great at sensing our moods and can pick up certain triggers to determine what we are about to do before we even do it.

I'll always remember Lady was such a clever girl and she always knew when we were going to go for a walk (I didn't even have to say the W-word…she just knew). Maybe it doesn't seem that clever just yet but let me explain.

Her lead lived in the cupboard under the stairs, and I could visit that cupboard 100 times a day and Lady would not even raise her head however when it came to walkies she was up and screeching in excitement before I even got that lead.

I experimented with this and practised going to the cupboard in different clothes, at different times of the day. One day I even went in my Harry Potter dressing gown (I'm very proud of the fact I own a Harry Potter dressing gown) and went to pick up her lead, but Lady did not move. She only got excited when it was in fact time to go for a walk. Now how did

Lady know? Especially when I had tried to trick her on several occasions?

She knew because she was able to read my body language, and clearly, there was something I was portraying through my body language to indicate it was time for a walk. Pretty clever right? Through learnt behaviour and repetition, Lady soon learnt what actions I was about to do before it was walkies time.

I also want to give you another example because another one-liner I hear all the time is "he knows, he knows he has done wrong". I hate to burst your bubble, but he doesn't know he has done wrong. I think this line is classically used when dogs have accidents in the house and the owners spot the accident way after it has happened and they speak to their dog like the dog understands English "whose done that? You bad lad!".

At this stage, the dog may cower or turn his head away from you, only looking at you from the corner of his eye (we call this whale eye). To most it would appear you shouting and pointing at that wee on the floor has an understanding from the dog but in fact, the dog isn't giving you that "guilty" look because he knows what he has done in fact he is responding to your body language and displaying calming signals so that you stop shouting at him and start being nice again.

If we were able to read our dog's body language, this would give us a massive advantage, far better than the other dog owners out there (the ones that haven't read this book of course!) and why? The answer is simple, being able to communicate and understand what our dog is trying to say will help us get them out of certain situations before they feel the need to bite and we have to remember when a dog chooses to bite this is the last resort, no dog wants to bite unless they feel there is no other option.

We call this **The Ladder of Aggression**

99% of bites could be avoided if we knew how to read the signs that our dogs were trying to portray. Dogs are faced with situations every day that can make them feel stressed or anxious. Recognising the signs will help prevent dogs from escalating up the 'ladder of aggression' and will help prevent dog bites.

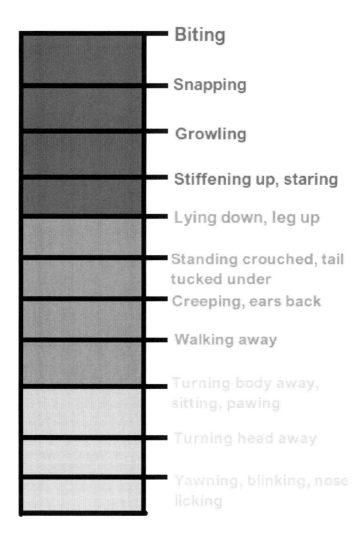

So what does the ladder of aggression actually mean? Basically, if you look at the bottom end of the ladder, yawning, blinking, nose licking these are classed as calming signals, and it's our dog's way of trying to say I am not very happy in this situation.

Sadly a lot of owners and other dogs, in fact, ignore these signals, so the dog is forced to elevate up the ladder which results in him trying to display another calming signal and if that is ignored (which it normally is) he will move up again, and he will keep moving up until he finds a behaviour that gets his a response i.e. the threat (the other dog) goes away.

Biting is at the top end of the ladder, and this is a last resort as dogs want to try all other options before getting to this stage, but sadly sometimes, they just are not given a chance. Biting takes up a lot of a dog's energy, but if he really feels like there is no other option, then he will use it.

Sadly there are so many cases reported of dogs biting children, but when you analyse the situation, you normally find that the dog was placed in a situation that he could not escape. This is one of the mean reasons I always advise giving your dog their own space (especially when you have children) and ensuring all interactions are supervised.

Once a dog finds a behaviour on the ladder of aggression that gets him the response he wants i.e. the threat goes away, he will use it every time he is faced with that threat. The higher up the ladder, the harder it is to correct (not impossible though, remember that!).

I find from experience people get in touch with me sadly when the dog has reached the top end of the ladder, basically when the owners have reached a crossroad, and they don't know what to do anymore!

If owners got in touch with me when their dog displayed behaviours at the lower end of the ladder life would be so much easier for me, the owner, and ultimately the dog involved. Do not get me wrong I would always encourage any owner to get in touch as sadly so many dogs end up in shelter due to behavioural issues and I hope this book helps and prevents dogs from ending up in shelter.

Now one thing I've seen happen in the past after meeting clients is, they take certain signals as gospel. I had one client ring me to say I'm really worried my dog is constantly yawning even when in the house does this mean he is stressed? I had another client say that her dog was licking his lips a lot in the house does this mean he is stressed?

Let us get one thing clear now when it comes to reading body language, you need to be able to read the full picture as well as taking into account the scenario! For example, if your dog is lying on the couch, curled up from a busy fun-packed day (like most of the dogs that attend our daycare) and then he yawns, chances are he is just tired.

If your dog has just had his tea and then licks his lips, chances are he is just making sure not a single crumb goes to waste.

If you imagine this scenario, your dog is in the park, and he has a group of dogs run over and surround him, sniffing him here, there and everywhere and then he yawns, licks his lips or turns his head…this is a calming signal HELP your dog out and get him out of that situation calmly before things escalate and don't be misled by certain forms of behaviour i.e. a wagging tail!

You could have a dog that is absolutely terrified and on the verge of a full-scale meltdown, and he will wag his tail. A wagging tail can mean a number of different things, and again to repeat what I have already said, you need to look at the full picture!

Not only is it important that you learn how to read your dog's body language but equally if you learn to read signals from other dogs it can also mean you can get your dog out of a possibly dangerous situation before things escalate.

Now as I am sure we are aware the breeds of dogs we have today range from tiny little Chihuahuas to giant Great Danes with lots of fluffy inbetweeners and some dogs are much harder to read than others. The hardest dog to read would be a brachycephalic breed (squished up face) such as an English Bull Dog, a Pug or a Shih Tzu. Not only are these breeds difficult for us to read, they are also very difficult for other dogs to read, which is sadly why these breeds are normally at the receiving end of a lot of fights.

They could be the most friendly and sociable dog in the world, but if another dog approaches and reads their body language the wrong way, it can have a devastating effect on them.

What we have to remember is brachycephalic breeds have all of the same features as a German Shepherd, but everything is squashed up giving them bulgy eyes, wrinkled skin, a stiff stance which to another dog could be seen as threatening behaviour hence why the other dog sadly retaliates.

The same can be said for black dogs or long-haired dogs with hair over their eyes as they too prove difficult for other dogs to read and sadly sometimes find themselves at the receiving end of a fight.

So how do we learn to "speak dog"? The answer is simple… use your eyes! Look at your dog's body language and facial expressions to see just how your dog is feeling. Having this ability will help keep you and your dog safe.

After being married for a number of years I have learnt how to read my wife's body language pretty well, that dark stare normally means…don't even think about it! That disapproving look normally means… too late he's done it just wait until the guests leave.

When it comes to being in trouble, I would say most men learn very quickly how to read a woman's body language, we have to, its an important part of our survival and it helps get us out of tricky situations. By learning to read your dog's body language, you too will be able to escape tricky situations.

Head to toe

When it comes to reading any dog's body language, you have to look from head to toe, some behaviours will be very subtle whilst others will be very prominent.

The friendly approach –

There are a number of behaviours a dog will display to suggest he wants to be friendly and interact with another dog. You need to learn to look at the full picture so for example a friendly dog will have a smooth forehead, he will make his approach sideways, his body will be relaxed, he may have squinty eyes, his ears will be back, and the insides of his ears will be visible (depending on the breed). Some dogs may even lift a paw and dip their head. These are all forms of communication and it is the dog's way of saying he means no harm and he comes in peace.

Fight, Freeze or flight

Just like us, dogs too will display a fight, freeze or flight when faced with a perceived threat. This is a physiological response that occurs within the body to prepare the body and most times, we just don't have any control over it.

Have you ever had someone come to you and hit you? How did you react? Did you stay still and do nothing? (FREEZE), Did you hit back? (FIGHT) or did you try to run away? (FLIGHT). These are all-natural responses and a response that we have little control over as it is our body's way of protecting us from potential threats or danger.

A freeze in a dog is also a warning sign, and it's the dog's way of preparing himself for what to do next. Sadly a lot of dogs have no option to fight because they are restricted i.e. they are on the lead, they have no way of escape. A freeze can be for a split second or can be for much longer and the behaviours he displays are completely different from that of a dog that wants to be friends.

This dog will have fixed staring eyes as he stares at the potential threat. You may also find that he has dilated pupils. His muzzle will be tightly closed, and it's not unusual for dogs to hold their breath. He may have a lowered body, and he will be keeping his head held low. Everything from head to toe will be tight and tense, and he will keep his ears back and down covering the insides.

Some dogs do prefer to move away from a situation to avoid conflict, and this is what we call the flight. Again, this dog will be displaying a number of signals to suggest he wants to run away from the situation. He will more than likely have a tucked tail; his weight will be pushed forward away from the threat. He will have a 'worried' look on his face and chances are his eyes will be wide. He may also have a hunched body and in some cases, he may be lifting a paw as a form of appeasement.

Now I am guessing your dog displays a fight response which is more than likely why you are reading this book, unless of course, you are in love with me... it's not uncommon! No doubt you will know exactly what your dog displays if he chooses to fight a situation. You may notice that he raises his lips to show as many teeth as he possibly can, as he snarls his muzzle will be wrinkled. His eyebrows will be drawn in, he may growl, he may bark. He will most definitely have a very hard stare at his perceived threat and chances are his ears will be held tightly back.

The stress signals!

Dog's are placed in stressful situations every day, and di
knowledge, we don't pick up on these early warning signals. If your dog
is stressed the most obvious thing he will do will be to yawn or lick his
lips however he may roll over to try and deflect the situation, his body
may be lowered, he may choose to look away from whatever it is that is
scaring him, he may shift his full weight to the back, he may raise his
paw. Certain male dogs when they get stressed may show arousal… in
other words, they will hump!

We have our own way of dealing with situations we are not comfortable
with for example my son, Harvey when in a situation he is not sure
about such as meeting new people will hide behind my leg and put his
thumb in his mouth. He will also avoid eye contact at all costs. We all
have our way of dealing with these situations we are faced with no matter
how old you are and although some may be down to the individual some
of the behaviours we humans display are very similar just as they are in
dogs.

The main thing to remember when it comes to us humans is we can
avoid awkward situations, we make our excuses and leave, but dogs do
not get this luxury. Dogs are forced into difficult situations every day,
and they can't make excuses, they cant remove themselves, they sadly
just have to get on with it, and that is how the ladder of aggression
comes into play.

I believe all owners should know how to read dog body language, that's
why we cover this topic in our training classes and why I include it within this book. If you can start to recognise behaviours in your dog, then I
can guarantee you will be able to help him as you will be armed with the
best tool any dog owner could have but sadly one most don't nor never
will have… the ability to speak dog!

Learn how to speak dog, and I can guarantee you will never look at a dog
the same again. I am forever analysing what a dog is thinking and trying
to communicate with me. When I go to client's homes, when I am out in
the park with my dog or down at the beach I am always watching and
reading dog's dog language.

t of the time it is because that's my job and I am unable to switch ff, but in a lot of situations, I get a lot of dogs running over to say hello to my dog Buddy. I am constantly watching the body language of the other dog as well as Buddy's, and if either display any signals to suggest they are not happy, then I do the responsible thing and separate them by taking Buddy away. Something so simple but it avoids a potential fight and it kept my dog safe.

Now that you are armed with this very valuable lesson, let us move on and look at active ways to help your dog with this behaviour.

Chapter Four

Helping them deal with the stresses life can throw at us

A lot of reactive dogs react out of fear and anxiety, and throughout this chapter, we will be looking at active ways that you can help reduce your dog's stress and anxiety levels and make them happier pooches.

Diet – you are what you eat!

We have all heard that phrase, and the same applies to our dogs. I always remember being a young lad and being told I couldn't eat the blue smarties… did you get that too?

These days we are constantly having healthy eating thrown in our face, it is on the TV, on the news, on social media, and why? The reason why is because it is better for us and helps us live longer, happier lives. We care (or should) about what we eat, and although I love my chocolate I do try and have a well-balanced diet, I write that with a box of celebrations by my side.

When it comes to dog food, there is such variation and so much conflicting information, how on earth do you know what to choose? I do not plan on telling you the ins and outs of diet foods available for dogs in this book, but one thing I would say is to avoid any diets that have meat or animal derivatives listed in their ingredients. These diets are normally classed as mixed formulated.

What is meant by the term meat and animal derivatives?

"Meat and animal derivatives are legally defined in the Animal Feed Regulations 2019. PFMA members use by-products of the human food industry that come from animals slaughtered under veterinary supervision eg. Heart, lung, or muscle meat, which may not be traditionally eaten by people in this country" – www.pfma.org.uk

Unfortunately, these diet foods normally equivalate to us eating fast food every day. Let us be honest fast food is normally quite yummy but long term that's not going to have a huge impact on our health and wellbeing and over time it's going to make us feel pretty rubbish and pretty sluggish. A lot of the ingredients found in cheaper dog foods are not of the highest quality and correct me if I am wrong, but we only want the best for our dog, right?

I would advise speaking to your veterinary practice, and I am sure they will help guide you in the right direction and help you make the right decision for your dog.

There are a number of diet foods available on the market specifically designed to help improve your dog's behaviour and to maintain an optimal emotional balance which in turn will help him overcome the day to day stresses life can have. These specific diets have all of the vital amino acids and vitamins required to synthesise the necessary neurotransmitters in a dog's brain to help promote calmness and relaxation.

Herbal remedies – to add a little extra calmness

Just like us, every now and then we may need something to help chill us out (no, I don't mean anything illegal!). There are a number of herbal remedies available for dogs that come in tablets, sprays, collars and plug ins to help them deal and cope with everyday life. These can be supplemented alongside your dog's diet and can have a number of benefits. It is important to remember, though, that these are not magic pills or sprays that cure-all. They are aimed to work alongside a training programme. Just like diet pills, if you read the small print, they require a healthy diet and exercise too

Choosing the right herbal remedy for your dog

If you go to your local pet shop, I am sure they will have a number of herbal remedies available which can be quite daunting, which one do you choose? If you go to one pet shop, you may be advised one thing, if you then visit another pet shop they may advise you something completely different.

I personally think the best place to go is your veterinary practice. The veterinary staff will all have had training regarding the products they are selling and chances are the staff will have used them on their dogs before... having worked in practice for a number of years I know vets, vet nurses and veterinary receptionists all have the 'problematic dogs'.

I would always prefer to give my dog something that has been advised by a veterinary practice because at the end of the day these guys have undergone a lot of training to be where they are and from my point of view, their opinion matters.

Of course, you can go on social media and ask everyone else for their opinion, but in all honesty, these guys are not vets or vet nurses.

Where do you go to get your car fixed? A mechanic! Where do you go if you are unwell? A doctor! Why is this? These are professionals in that field and although I am sure the people you ask on social media may generally want to help, let's be honest they are not veterinary trained. As a canine behaviourist, I only recommend products that can be purchased from a veterinary practice and having used them myself with my dogs in the past, I know they help.

Let us get one thing clear though, introducing herbal remedies to your dog's diet is not going to correct the problem; certainly it may help, but it won't stop your dog from wanting to attack every other dog it sees. The idea of herbal remedies is to help reduce your dog's anxiety so that you can introduce changes and a training plan to help correct the problem.

Learn to earn programme – Because nothing in life is free!

In order to teach your dog something new and in order to move forward, we must begin by teaching our dog that if he wants something, he has to do something in order to get it.

Answer me this! Why do you go to work? You may be lucky like me, and you may love your job but let's be completely honest we go to work for one thing, and that's the pay packet at the end of the month. In order to get that pay packet, we have to work for it and why?...because nothing in life is free.

The Nothing in life is free programme is kind of like teaching your child to say please or thank you, something most parents do with their children from an early age. The more your dog works for something, the more he is going to want the result.

Here are some examples

1. Feeding your dog - don't just put his bowl of food down make him work for it! For example, he can sit, lie down, give a paw, but he must do something in order to get that reward.
2. Taking him for a walk – don't just put his lead on, make him work for that reward of going for a walk. For example, he can sit or stay before getting the lead put on him. When it comes to opening the front door ask him to do something first and then once he has done it the reward is him going outside. I do not care who walks out of the door first (If you insist on going out first then I hate to break it to you but you are wasting your time, your dog doesn't care and if he is that excited you are just going to get tripped up!)
3. Playing with toys – Don't just throw the ball make him work for it. For example, ask him to sit, and once he has throw the ball (that's the reward!). If he brings it back, ask him to leave it, and if he does, REWARD him for it.

The thing to remember is if your dog is going to get a positive outcome, he must work for it first. This is the foundation of his training, and you must follow in order for any further training to work.

Attention seeking behaviours

Dogs are great at getting our attention and us humans just make it so easy for them. We need to try and give our dog more confidence and independence and to do that we must ignore any attention-seeking behaviours.

I am going to stress now I am not saying you cannot love your dog or give him any attention, just the thought of that sounds horrible. Instead, I want this attention to be on your terms so, for example, I am sat watching TV at night time (I'll not lie I'm not a sports guy it would be the soaps for me) and let us just say Buddy starts jumping up at me. That would be attention on his terms, and I must ignore it.

There are three rules to remember when ignoring any unwanted behaviours:-

1. Do not look at your dog
2. Do not speak to your dog
3. Do not touch your dog.

If you do any of those, then you may as well put your dog on their back and stroke their belly and praise them for looking cute.

You may find that your dog's attention-seeking behaviours get worse before it gets better, but you must remember we are doing this for your dog's benefit as we want our dogs to be more confident and we want our dogs to have more independence.

Let us say I have ignored Buddy for 1 hour, and he eventually gives up and starts to go towards his bed, then and only then if I wanted to, I could call him to me and I could spend the remaining of the night giving him cuddles, kisses... you know the things us dog owners do! By doing that I have now given my dog attention on my terms.

Routine – Because dog's love to know what is next

Let us be honest us humans work well to a routine, and I personally get lost when my routine is broken. We all have our own little routines for certain things such as what you do once you wake up in a morning, which order you put your clothes on (socks always before trousers...am I right?), your bedtime routine. Whatever it is and as much as you try to deny it we all have our own little routines that we stick to without even realising. Dogs, like us, work well in a routine.

There will be some that argue against that, but I have worked with dogs for a number of years, and I have seen the benefits of placing your dog in a routine. A routine for dogs should consist of five things, however, certain parts of a routine should be varied to prevent causing boredom. Let me explain.

1. Set Meal times.

A lot of owners choose to feed their dog on demand and leave food out all day long. This is perhaps the more convenient option as people need to go to work, it's easier just to know he has it if he wants it. I personally believe it is far more beneficial to have set meal times for your dog, and I look at it from a veterinary nurses point of view.

Appetite is a great indicator of health, if your dog stops eating chances are there might be something wrong with him that requires medical attention. If your dog grazes, it will make it far more difficult to pick up on any early signals.

I think having set meal times also prevents unwanted pests making it a much more hygienic option for your dog.

From a trainer and behaviourist's point of view, I find set meals help with maintaining good toilet habits as you can roughly guess what sort of time your dog needs to poop. I also think set meal times are a great way to offer training opportunities and help reinforce that learn to earn programme – nothing in life is free!

I would advise getting your dog to work for his food (sadly I do not mean doing the housework, washing the car of getting in the weekly shop) for example asking him to sit and stay until you release him. This will make his food appear more valuable as now he has had to work for it.

If you were given £50 every day just for the sake of it, eventually you would lose the value of that money but because you have to work throughout the week and throughout the month to get that pay package it always seems more valuable to you, even if you are like me and spend it within a few days of it reaching the bank.

I personally am not a fan of food bowls and would always recommend that you mix up your dog's feeding by introducing brain games to encourage your dog to work harder for his food resulting in giving your dog adequate mental stimulation (something equally as important as exercise).

2. Exercise

Believe it or not, dog's need DAILY exercise and a walk around the block does not count as exercise, nor does that 'BIG' back garden you may have. Dog's need to go out and actually be walked and you can't be a weather depending sort of person when it comes to your dog.

Your dog needs to be walked every day come rain or shine! As discussed above, certain parts of a dog's routine should be varied, and exercise should definitely be varied. This means dogs need to go to different locations and not just be given the same boring walk every day.

I personally would get bored, never mind the dog. I like to go to new places to explore and my dog Buddy loves new locations. Taking your dog to new locations encourages them to make use of their natural senses i.e. they see different things, they smell different things, they hear different things, they touch different things.

Making use of your dog's natural senses is a great form of mental stimulation, and it helps keep your dog happy and content, which in turn helps reduce your dog's anxiety levels.

Walks don't just need to be on a lead, it is important that you get your dog off lead (maybe not around dogs at this moment if your dog can be reactive) to help burn some excess energy off him. There is nothing more rewarding than seeing a dog off lead, running and doing what dogs should be doing – having fun!

There are lots of private fields available for you to hire to give your dog that opportunity if you are worried about coming into an encounter with another dog or maybe your dog's training, isn't that reliable. I recently visited Dogwood Adventure Play in Stockton-On-Tees.

Dogwood offers two enclosed private fields equipped with tunnels, climbing frames, logs, swimming pools, sensory gardens and seven acres of countryside. These are purpose-built fields that can be hired out on an individual basis all year round. They are ideal for dogs that cannot be let off the lead in public places and great if you do not want to encounter any other dogs. Check out their website www.dogwoodadventureplay.com

As hard as it is to believe, some dogs get no exercise or only get walked on a weekend when everyone is off work. Imagine how you would feel being stuck in your house every day with no Television, no books and no mobile phone. How long do you think it would take before you cracked up?

It may be nice for the first 1-2 hours having some peace and quiet, but then boredom will kick in, and before long you will start to feel pretty fed up. We know this, yet some people find it acceptable for our dogs and then wonder why their dog develop training and behaviour issues. The top and bottom of it is you MUST get your dog out for a decent walk every day and if you can't then look at employing a dog walker because trust me your dog needs this.

3. Training times

In an ideal world, dogs should get 3-4 training sessions per day, and each session should be around 5-10 minutes. I would advise always starting the training session with something you know your dog can perform reliably i.e. the sit, and always end the session with something you know your dog can perform reliably.

In between start teaching your dog something new and this can be anything you like. There are so many books and resources available to help you (Just make sure what you read only promotes positive based methods of training!) and set training time is a great way to establish a nice bond between you and your dog.

Set training time also helps to reinforce that nothing in life is a free programme, and it is also a great form of mental stimulation.

Believe it or not, mental stimulation is a great way to help reduce anxiety in your dog as well as help burn off excess energy. It will tire a dog out more to mentally stimulate him than it would to physically stimulate him i.e take him for a walk.

In fact, a 10-minute training session is equivalent to a 45 minute on-lead walk, but it is important to remember the two need to work hand in hand together. If you would like a starting point with your dog's training, then check out the bonus section at the end of the book.

Alongside training times, I would also advise set brain games, for example puzzle games to encourage your dog to use their brain. Bear in mind you do not need to be spending a fortune you can also make your own (a little something I like to call recycle the recycling).

Basically, this means if you are about to throw something in the bin before you do can it be used as a brain game for your dog? It does not matter if the dog destroys it, it's going in the bin anyways right?

The more you train your dog and the more forms of mental stimulation you provide for your dog, the happier they will be. Do not forget this part of a dog's routine should also be varied i.e. do not just focus on the same training and do not keep providing the same old brain games – your dog will get bored and lose interest.

4. Play Time

This is a great way to bond with your dog, as dogs love our attention. This should be yours and your dog's time together to play and enjoy each others company. In an ideal world, we would have 3-4 playtime sessions per day each session lasting around 5-10 minutes but if you have the 'time' to offer more playtime sessions, I am sure your dog will not object.

I am sure your dog has a basket of toys, am I right? How many does he actually play with? I would advise having a few toys out at any one time and rotating them every couple of days to keep things interesting for your dog.

I would also keep a couple of his favourite toys to one side, and they should only come out during playtime, which will help make the game much more fun. Do not forget the main rule, nothing in life is free if your dog wants to play; they have to work for it first.

Some dogs prefer rag toys whilst others prefer balls and others prefer squeaky toys. Find a toy that you know you and your dog can have lots of fun with and remember to vary the toys you use to keep your dog interested and focused.

Do not forget if you are playing a game of tug with your dog to let them win from time to time. Personally, I hate losing, I am quite a competitive person, especially when it comes to Monopoly. My strategy is simple, get as many hotels as possible and take everyone else's money. You may have heard of games of Monopoly ending with the board game being thrown across the room... that's me... I hate to lose.

Every Tuesday I go to my friend's house for games night. There are normally six of us, and we spend the night playing games and having a laugh which is always great fun. I go in with the I'm going to win attitude but sometimes I don't win.

Just because I loose occasionally I know sometimes I'm going to win and it's the thrill of the unknown that encourages me to go every week. I probably wouldn't get bored if I lost every week (probably just angry) and it probably wouldn't stop me from going but for dogs in order to keep them interested they need to win from time to time as they need to get the thrill of that reward because that will encourage them to want to play next time.

5. Quiet Time

Like us dogs need time to unwind, put their paws up and forget about the worries the day may have brought. It is important that we allow our dogs to get quiet time throughout the day to sleep and it is equally important that they have their own space that they can go to if they wish i.e. their own bed.

It is important to remember when they are in their space that they do not get disturbed; this is their area and their time to relax. At our Daycare centre, all of our dogs go down for naps throughout the day away from the other dogs as it is important, they get the chance to rest.

What happens to us if we have a bad night sleep? We wake up grumpy, we are grouchy, we become very argumentative, we slam doors, we moan about how tired we are, and in general we are just not the nicest of people to be around. Have you ever encountered an overly tired toddler?

They bite, kick and scream, but it's not their fault really, they are just overly tired. Overtired dogs are a little bit like overtired toddlers in the fact they too can act problematically, but when they get tired, there is a high chance they can bite and going back to that ladder of aggression once they realise that biting works then they will use it time and time again so make sure your dog gets a little bit ME time to relax and really stretch those legs out.

I can't tell you how to live your life or when you should walk your dog or train your dog; this is your life and your routine. As a family, you need to sit down and share the responsibilities between you, and it may involve getting up a bit earlier in the morning to offer an extra walk or a little training session but just remember you are doing this for one main reason – the happiness of your dog!

Throughout this chapter, we have discussed a number of ways to help reduce your dog's anxiety, and there is one thing left to discuss to neuter or not to neuter?

From a Veterinary Nurse's point of view, I would always advise getting your dog neutered, and when I used to work in practice, the standard recommended age was 6 months however due to new evidence certain things have changed for certain breeds i.e. larger breeds.

There are a number of health benefits to getting your dog neutered for example it helps reduce unwanted cancers, prevents unwanted seasons, litters (let's be honest there are already lots of dogs in the world, sadly lots without homes we don't need to add to that), prevents your dog from straying, prevents dog theft etc.

Will neutering help your reactive dog?

Personally, I would not advise neutering an already nervous dog as in a lot of cases neutering has made the problem worse, but in all fairness, the behaviours your dog is displaying is learnt behaviour i.e. the dog has learnt that this behaviour gets rid of the problem so, for example, the dog barks, lunges, growls, bares his teeth and the dog walks away.

Neutering is not going to suddenly make him forget to change his perception of other dogs and to recondition his unwanted behaviours. The dog will require training and that is what we will be discussing in the next chapter.

I would advise helping to reduce your dog's anxiety then correcting your dog's unwanted behaviours around other dogs and then once life is sweet and smelling of roses again then we can look at neutering him as ultimately I do think there are a number of benefits for your dog which will help them live a long and comfortable life.

Chapter Five

'Look at me'

Although you may think we have reached the main part of the book (how to correct this unwanted behaviour) the main ways to stop and control these unwanted behaviours began in Chapter One. Only when you know why a dog is reacting the way he is can you correct it. Once you know why you then need to be able to recognise certain signals your dog may express through his body language in order to help him get out of tricky situations. In order to implement a new training programme, you need to make sure measures are put into place to help reduce his anxiety.

Once you have worked through Chapter 1-4 NOW you are ready to introduce a desensitisation programme. This is basically a technique that involves exposing the dog to the previously threatening situation i.e. another dog but exposing the dog to the stimulus in a much more relaxed and controlled environment until the anxiety reaction we currently see disappears.

We have to remember that when a dog is frightened, it is not his fault, he cannot help it, but as an owner, we have a responsibility to ensure our dog is as happy and relaxed as he can be. Just like us, it is perfectly normal for a dog to be frightened of something, but if this something is having an impact on his day to day life and stopping him doing what he loves to do i.e. go for a walk, something has to change.

Back in 2018, I received my acceptance letter to visit Hogwarts and become a wizard. Unfortunately, it turns out I can't actually fly a broom very well, I did not know any spells, and I did not have a magic wand.

My dreams were crushed, but at least I still had my dazzling good looks. Now if you are honest you too don't have a magic wand, and so I need you to remember this part - Training and behaviour modification programmes take time and patience and a lot of hard work.

So the questions I am sure you have all be waiting to hear the answer to, is how do I build up a positive association around other dogs?

The answer is simple 'LOOK AT ME'

We are going to attempt to change the way your dog feels when they see another dog so instead of feeling the need to react, jump, lunge, bark, growl etc. we are going to change all of the behaviours to one simple behaviour, and that is getting your dog to look at you in anticipation for a reward.

In order to build up a reliable 'look at me' cue, we need to start in an area of little distraction (your home). At this early stage, it is vital that we avoid all other dogs (I am sure you do your best to do that anyways) as best as we can and it is equally important that we do not use the look at me cue outside around other dogs just yet otherwise we risk building up a negative association to the cue 'look at me.'

We need to devote some time each day to practice stage one of the 'look at me' cue (This could be part of your training times, as discussed in the previous chapter).

The best time to practice is when both you and your dog are relaxed. I want you to get some extra high-value treats, something that your dog would not normally have but something he is really going to want to work for.

Have your dog sit in front of you and wait patiently until he turns his head away from you. As soon as he does bring the treat to your eyes and say the cue 'look at me'. As soon as the dog's head turns and looks at you, praise him immediately (within 2 seconds).

The key to success is repeat, repeat and then repeat some more. I cannot stress enough how important it is that you only use the 'look at me' cue indoors to begin with. In order to move on to phase two, we need to make sure we are consistently achieving the results set out in stage one i.e. your dog looks at you every time he hears the 'look at me' cue.

Every dog is different, just like us and like us, we learn at different levels. Some dogs pick things up very easily, but others can take a little longer. Try not to push your dog too hard and certainly do not get frustrated if they do not do it straight away or as quickly as you would like them to. I always advise not putting a time limit on your training, if it takes a few days great but if it takes a few months, that's also fine.

When you feel your dog is performing the 'look at me' cue reliably 100% of the time, then you can safely and happily move onto stage two of the training.

Stage two involves upping the level of distraction, but it is important to remember that I still do not want you practising the 'look at me' on walks around other dogs. What we need to do is start practising in the garden or back yard or even the back lane (depending on where you live). In the garden, there are more smells, more noises and ultimately more distractions than you had in stage one.

By now your dog should know the 'look at me' cue, and he should know that if he looks at you something yummy is coming his way, if not then you should not have moved onto stage two and I would advise you going back a step and practising some more with stage one.

When in the garden allow your dog to have a sniff around, keep him on the lead so that he does not wander too far as remember to have a reliable 'look at me' cue he needs to be close enough so that you can praise immediately. When having a sniff practice with the 'look at me' cue and as soon as he looks give him that yummy treat.

Hopefully, he looked at you but if not never be afraid to go back a step. We want the results, and in order to get those results, we need to take our time and build it up gradually. I would also advise at this stage varying the treats you use (still keeping them of high value) to help keep it interesting for your dog. You can also use his favourite toy if he responds better to that.

As in stage one, in order to get a reliable 'look at me,' you need to repeat, repeat and then repeat some more. Only when he is looking at you 100% of the time during the training sessions can you then move onto stage three.

As in stage two, we now need to up that level of distraction, and now we are going to practice the 'look at me' on his walks. However, I still want you to avoid all other dogs at this stage or as best as you can and to stress once again please do not attempt the 'look at me' cue around another dog no matter how good he was at stages one and two. If you do encounter other dogs, then all you need to do is get him out of that situation as quickly and as safely as you possibly can.

Stage three is a little bit more difficult because there are a lot more distractions outside in the big open world and what we want to achieve is for your dog to look at you whenever he hears the cue. You need to practice in different areas i.e. the street, the park, the beach but starting with quieter areas, to begin with, and gradually building it up. You may find that this stage takes a lot longer than stages one and two, which is fine because remember there is no rush and Rome was not built in a day.

When walking down the street, allow your dog to sniff, look around and every now and then issue the 'look at me' cue and keep everything crossed that he looks at you. To guarantee he will, try adjusting the tone of your voice so that it sounds fun and enthusiastic rather than military-style... I would not look at someone if they were shouting, screaming at me.

Again I want you to keep varying the treats to keep him interested and focused. Over time slowly start to increase the level of distraction when outside so that we can eventually (remember no time limit) reach stage four.

Stage four is the stage I am sure you will not be looking forward too, as this is the stage where we are going to actively start looking for other dogs. We are now aiming to achieve that desensitisation process we discussed at the beginning of the chapter, and we are going to start aiming to recondition these unwanted behaviours to that of a more acceptable behaviour. This stage is perhaps the most crucial, and it is so important that you take your time and focus on your timing.

So where do you need to start?

You need to find somewhere that you and your dog can stand where you can see another dog, but your dog is NOT reacting. This could be a big field, it could be the beach, or it could be ten blocks away. It doesn't matter how far away you are initially as long as your dog can see another dog. This is where your hard work will pay off with the previous training you have been doing with the 'look at me' cue.

Once you find a place where your dog is calm and non-reacting, you now need to wait until he looks at the other dog. As soon as he does, you need to issue the 'look at me' cue and keeping those fingers and toes crossed, hoping that he looks at you. As soon as he does give him his reward and lots of praise. Remember this is so impressive that your dog has been able to control himself this way so he deserves the best of treats.

Every time he looks at the other dog, you need to issue the cue 'look at me' and then give him a treat. If he looks at that other dog in the distance 100 times then theoretically, he should have been issued 100 treats. This is why it is so important that you take a lot of treats out with you initially. Do not be tight when it comes to treats and expect to give him a lot at the beginning stages, just make sure you reduce his daily allowance of food to compensate for these extra goodies.

Now I don't want to be responsible for your dog getting the shits and making a mess all over the house so I would advise varying the high-value food to avoid upset stomachs and stay clear of dairy products. I find chicken or ham works really well.

As with previous stages, the key to success is repetition. I know you will be edging to move forward but only move forward when you feel you are ready and ultimately when you feel your dog is ready.

It is important at this stage of the training that you remember if you happen to come into encounter with a dog closer than the distance you have been practising do not use the 'look at me' as again this could build up a negative association to the cue.

We are aiming at desensitising your dog around other dogs, and that takes time, lots of patience and consistency so, for example, make sure you watch your dog at all times and be sure to issue the 'look at me' cue the second his head turns towards another dog.

Over time the aim is to slowly reduce the distance between you and the other dog no one gets a medal for being the fastest in this form of training. Slow and steady always wins the race!

If say you began by being 100 metres away from another dog and you feel your dog has responded well and you decide to half that distance and all of a sudden your dog starts to react problematically do not throw the towel in. Accept that things do not happen overnight, and never be afraid to go back a step because at the end of the day we need to make sure that our dog is ready to progress on to the next stage.

Now in days, weeks or even months you will slowly be able to decrease that distance. I think it is important to point out I do not expect you to take a tape measure out on your walks with you, just use your own judgment. At this stage in your dog's training, it may be worth having a look back at Chapter Three to remind yourself of certain forms of body language your dog may display. If he is not feeling happy and if you notice your dog displaying these, then get him out of that situation quickly and safely before behaviours begin to escalate.

If you do this correctly, over time you will be moving closer and closer towards another dog and eventually, you will be able to walk past another dog.

Let us think of a real-life situation

You are walking down the street, and you see another dog heading your way with their owner, your gut will be screaming at you to cross the road or run and hide but remember all of the hard work you have already achieved with your dog.

As you walk towards the other dog keep watching your dog and as soon as he looks at the other dog issue the 'look at me' cue. Remember the golden rule, every time he looks at the other dog; you need to be ready to get his focus back on you.

I have done numerous 1-1 behaviour appointments with clients, and I find the biggest issue is people's timings and unfortunately this is the most important thing that needs to be spot on in order for this desensitisation programme to work and get the results that you need. Following that is time, patience and consistency... without them, you will not get the results you want.

Fed up of seeing the words time, patience and consistency yet? Don't worry I will repeat it a lot more as the book goers on.

Dogs are such clever little creatures and pick things up very easily if you reward the behaviour at the correct moment. Just remember treat to repeat, and you won't go wrong.

Eventually and after some training, your dog will start to automatically look up at you when they see another dog before you have even had a chance to say the look at me cue. At this point in time you may feel the need to contact me to say thank you so much and by all means, feel free to. In all honesty, you deserve a good pat on the back because you have now successfully achieved what you set out to do at the beginning of the book and you have helped desensitise your dog but the training does not stop there, we still have a few more things to cover which we will be moving onto in Chapter Six.

Summary of the 'Look at me'

The purpose of the 'look at me' cue is to desensitise your dog towards other dogs under a relaxed and controlled situation. You need to begin by teaching the 'look at me' cue indoors where there is very little distraction and only when your dog is ready will you progress onto stage two which involves increasing the level of distraction and practising in the garden or back lane.

When your dog is ready, you can start practising in the streets, on walks but still avoiding any encounters with other dogs just yet. If you do encounter any other dogs at the early stages and your dog does react, just get him out of that situation as quickly and calmly as you can. When you feel your dog looks at you 100% of the time, you can then move onto stage four which involves looking for other dogs.

We position ourselves with our dog at a distance from another dog (where your dog is non-reactive), and we wait patiently until your dog looks at the other dog. As soon as he does issue the 'look at me' cue and praise immediately (within 2 seconds).

Over time we will reduce the distance between our dog and the other dog, remembering this can take days, weeks or even months (do not put a time stamp on your dog's training!).

Eventually, after some time, patience and you guessed it, consistency we will be at a stage where we can walk past another dog and every time your dog looks at the other dog, we issue the 'look at me' cue and praise our dog with a treat for doing so.

Now you have achieved the desensitisation programme and successfully build up a positive association around other dogs. As we know, life always throws spanners into the works so we need to be prepared for times when the 'look at me' will not work, and that takes us onto the next chapter.

Chapter Six

Turn Around

There will always be that time when the 'look at me' cue is just not going to work. Maybe your dog gets taken by surprise, and before you even get a chance to issue the command, his emotions have gone through the roof.

Imagine this, how would you feel if you were walking down the road and out of nowhere 100 spiders come crawling around the corner straight for you with no warning and no way of escape, how do you react? Do you calmly walk past or do you scream bloody Mary? I know what I would do. We always have surprises around every corner but we cannot let these surprises put an end to the hard work we have already achieved; otherwise, what is the point?

Let me tell you a story about the time I was trapped in a room with four lovely ladies. I took some of our canine carers to an escape room as a team bonding session. For those that do not know what an escape room is, basically, it is a game where you get locked in a room for 1 hour, and you have a number of clues and codes to crack in order to escape before the time runs out.

This was the first escape room I had done, and I did not know what to expect. We were placed in a room which appeared fairly simple, and we had four padlocks on the door to which we believed was the exit.

We worked together as a team, and our communication was very impressive at the beginning stages. After the first 20 minutes, we had unlocked three of the four padlocks, and I for one, was feeling fairly confident that we were going to escape.

We had 16 minutes to spare, and we found the final code for the final padlock to get us out of the room. However, there was a surprise around the corner, and when we opened up the door, we were faced with another room which was filled with more padlocks, more clues and panic completely set in. We lost any form of communication we had, we stopped working together and we were running around like headless chickens trying our hardest to escape.

Unfortunately, we did not escape, and the time ran out, but it is safe to say we had a lot of fun along the way. The moral of the story is surprises lurk around every corner (or every closed door) and how you cope with these surprises is of utter importance. You could be like us and go straight into panic mode or you can have a plan B already prepared to help you and your dog get to 'safety'.

Plan B involves turning around and getting your dog somewhere safe. (Just think Bonnie Tyler, Turn around, bright eyes)

To achieve plan B, we must as always be prepared to put in the work. To begin, we need to start in an area of low distraction just as we did when teaching the 'look at me' we want to start at home where you and your dog are the only show in town.

Place your dog on his lead, have some of them yummy treats to hand and start walking (this works better in a long corridor) to the opposite end of the room.

As you reach the other end of the corridor, using your treat lure your dog around and as he follows say the cue 'turn' and once he has turned 180 degrees and is facing the opposite direction give him his yummy treat and tell him he is a good boy. As always, to build up a reliable action you guessed it, we must repeat, repeat and then repeat some more.

Walk from one end of the corridor to another and keep practising the turn cue. Once your dog has mastered it we can now start incorporating steps after the turn as let's be honest there would be no benefit in turning around at a corner and then stopping still the idea is to help get the dog a safe distance from the other dog without any dramas.

So now we repeat the turn, but this time once your dog has turned, we withhold the treat and take one step forward, and then we praise the dog with his treat and a 'good boy'. Repeat this stage a few times and then start to get the dog to walk two steps and then three steps before getting the treat. The idea is to get your dog to walk as many steps as possible after he has turned around before he gets the treats.

Now we can start to practice outside on our walks to help us build up to a real-life situation. I would not advise practising on corners where you cannot see around in fear of it actually being a real-life situation at this stage. Instead, I would say practice in quiet areas just to be 100% sure your dog will respond when you issue the cue.

Repeat, repeat and then (yes you have guessed it) repeat some more and when you feel your dog is confidently displaying the turn, you can now build up to a real-life situation.

Being prepared is the golden rule with this stage (not forgetting time, patience and consistency of course) of your dog's training and you need to be alert and on guard ready to dive into action if needed. Therefore, put your phone away and try to remain focused on your dog. As you approach a corner that you cannot see round think to yourself

1. WHAT
2. WHERE
3. WHEN

So number 1, what are you going to do if you have a dog-dog collision at this corner? Number 2, where are you going to go to get your dog to a safe distance away from the dog? Number 3, when do you need to decide?

Number 1 is simple because this is what we have been building up to. If we have a dog-dog collision, we are simply going to issue the cue 'turn' and turn our dog and walk away from the problem. Number 2, where are we going to go? This needs to be planned in your head before you arrive at the corner and you need to be looking at your surroundings.

Imagine this you are walking towards your corner; you have a busy main road to one side of you, this should be immediately removed from the equation of WHERE because you cannot guarantee that you can get across that road safely and quickly without causing an accident. You always have the direction you just came from (not ideal, but if it's the only option you have to keep your dog happy and safe, then what are you waiting for?). You may be lucky and have a nice little grass patch set aside from the pavement.

Let us imagine you have that little grass patch and that is where you have decided to go should a situation arise. Now you are all prepared you just need to remember WHEN and the answer is simple as soon as you encounter another dog at a corner act immediately.

So we are all prepared now for approaching our corner (let's hope it is a long street as that took some thinking!) and imagine that as you reach your corner, you are faced with another owner and their dog. No time to say hello, you need to act immediately and cue your dog to turn. As soon as he does, we would lead him to that little grass patch that is sitting so conveniently just off the pavement. As you reach the grass patch, you can praise your dog with his yummy treat and a good boy for his turn and steps.

Now, this is the important part; if he now looks back at the dog, make use of the 'look at me' cue and as soon as he looks back at you treat and praise. Remember though if he looks at that dog 20 times, he should have 20 treats inside his belly.

It is important at this stage to say that it is not just corners you need to be aware of. When you are out with your dog, you need to be aware of your full surroundings, don't just focus on what is straight ahead. You need to have aeroplane eyes and be prepared for that dog that comes running out of nowhere.

Summary of the Turn

Dog's like to be helped out from time to time, and it has been proven that they like to be helped out of stressful situations. Sometimes events occur that are out of our hands such as a dog – dog collision at a corner, but that's ok as now we know what we need to be doing, and the answer is simple, turn around and walk away (anyone else singing Bonnie Tyler right now?)

Start practising at home with just the turn command, to begin with, and once your dog reliably displays the perfect turn, you can now start to incorporate steps before giving him his treat. The aim is to walk as many steps as possible before treating.

We can now start practising on our walks and building up to a real-life situation just remember the three rules 1. What do I do? The answer is simply turn around and walk away. 2. Where do I go? This needs to be planned before you reach the corner; otherwise, the whole plan will go down the drain. 3. When you need to react? Immediately!

This is, of course, a technique you use only on that what-if factor and you may never have to use it (fingers crossed you don't), but it is always advisable to have a plan B in place and ready just in case because as I already mentioned if I turned a corner and I was faced with 100 spiders, I would go straight into panic mode but I would be grateful for a bit of help getting me out of that situation.

I would say moving forward we must remember that we need to be alert and ready to react in certain situations because this is how we can help our dog and get them to a safe area where he feels more relaxed, hence making the look at me cue much easier for your dog to do.

Chapter Seven

It's ok, my dog's friendly

How many times have you been out on a walk with your dog and another dog comes bounding over with a frantic owner in the background shouting "it's ok, my dog's friendly" Well that's great to hear, but my dog on the lead may not be hence why he is on a lead.

I enjoy my walks with Buddy and sometimes I just want it to be me and Buddy, don't get me wrong I do allow Buddy to play because that is his favourite thing to do, but sometimes I just want to be alone and work on Buddy's lead training, recall or just having some fun with him and I do not always want to be disturbed by other dog owners, whether their dog is friendly or not.

Personally, I think it is bad manners, and it is not showing any signs of respect with the fact your dog is on the lead, and he may need space. Do not get me wrong I never blame the dog running over, the issue lies with the owner, however many miles away from you.

So what do we do when that big excitable Labrador comes running over to say hello? We need to have a plan!

Now common sense would tell you if you are walking your dog and you come across a group of dogs off lead running wild...turn and run away! I do, however, appreciate that sometimes that off lead dog can appear from nowhere, which is why we need to be ready to act fast!

So what do you do?

You need to position yourself between your dog and the excitable dog running towards you. You need to ask your dog to sit and stay as you walk the stretch of your dog's lead. This is harder than it sounds as dogs will naturally follow when the lead pulls (well most of them) therefore you need to be working on your dog's sit and stay, and this begins indoors where there are little distractions.

1. Start in a low-level distraction area. Tell your dog to "sit" (which you reward them for), and slowly lean back from them whilst showing them your hand in a flat upright position. Whilst doing this cue "stay". If your dog comes towards you, do not reward. Keep repeating this step several times until your dog stays every time. ALWAYS return to your dog to give them a treat rather than asking them to come to you.
2. Once you can lean back from your dog and they can stay, take one step away from them following the same rules as before. If your dog does this, reward them and keep repeating this step until perfected. If they come to you while doing this step, repeat stage one again.
3. Slowly build up how far away you go from your dog for the stay command, remembering to always go back to them and reward them for staying.

The aim of the game is to build up how long you can ask your dog to stay for before returning. Once you are confident that your dog will stay, then you need to up the game. Dog's focus a lot of our body language, which makes the next part a little tricky as now we need to request a stay whilst we keep our back to our dog.

I always laugh when I practice this with owners during 1-1 appointments as so many dogs run in front of their owners as soon as they turn their back. This is due to the fact that dogs learn to read our body language from the front. Patience is key as always, and to help get it right we need to turn around gradually.

If your dog is demonstrating a brilliant and reliable sit/stay (he should be, or you are not ready to move on), then he should recognise the raised flat palm as a signal to mean STAY.

I want you to repeat the above steps but this time as you back away from your dog do so at a slight angle and over time you are going to increase that angle so that you are 180 degrees facing away from him. During this gradual build-up, make sure your dog can always see that flat palm as that will help to reinforce the behaviour you are trying to achieve.

Now that part is out of the way, we can now start to build up to a real-life situation which involves practising in an area of higher distraction i.e. the park, the beach (do not do this around off lead dogs). With this form of training, although it is a 'what-if' scenario we need to be prepared and make sure our dog displays the behaviour as soon as we ask, which is why we need to repeat, repeat and then repeat some more (I think you are catching on by now).

Going back to that excitable Labrador that is bounding towards us with his owner screaming "it's ok, he is friendly" in the background we now need to act fast. We need to place our dog in the sit/stay position and walk the stretch of his lead.

We need to reach into our pockets for a handful of them high value treats and get the excitable Labrador's attention. Now I don't care how you do this (just don't jump up and down naked...I don't want to be responsible for your arrest) but make sure that dog is focused on you and the treats you have.

You are now going to throw the treats as far away as possible, keeping everything crossed the Labrador runs for them and as soon as he does this is where you and your dog make your great escape!

Trust me when I say some dogs will not give a monkeys what you have to offer they will be more interested in seeing your dog, so this is where we need another plan of action. Now we introduce the continuous feed, and this involves getting down on your knees (oooh steady on!) and liter-ally giving your dog treat after treat until the owner of the other dog fi-nally catches up.

At this point, you can say whatever you feel like saying to that other owner (I will not judge), and once that other dog has been put on the lead, then you can walk calmly away with your dog.

Common sense would say to try and avoid all dogs off lead during this full training process, but I do appreciate that sometimes dogs just appear out of nowhere, which is why I find this a useful training tool to have under your belt.

Summary of the sit/stay in an emergency situation

Expecting your dog to be calm when faced with an impossible situation is a real challenge, and although the main focus of this type of training is the 'look at me' cue we need to have contingency plans for when we know the 'look at me' is not going to work.

This type of training requires (do I really have to say it again) training, patience and consistency. Eventually, after lots of training, you should be able to ask your dog to sit and stay whilst you turn your back to him and face the upcoming dog. Offering treats to the other dog is a great way to get his attention whilst you make your great escape with your dog.

We cannot expect our dog to respond to the 'look at me' command when he is faced with a situation like this which is why we have Plan B ready to use as and when necessary.

Chapter Eight

Your goal for success

Now that you have received all of the information you need to move forward with your dog, it is now time to start taking action.

You need to look at ways of reducing your dog's anxiety by following the advice given in this book. That may involve supplementing your dog with herbal remedies or looking at a potential diet change. Please remember these methods are not designed to change your dog's behaviour but more to give a helping hand to help reduce your dog's anxiety whilst you implement your new training plan.

Remember nothing in life is free and if you want to get the best from your dog, you need to implement this new programme to help build up confidence and independence and in turn reduce your dog's anxiety. This must be implemented by everyone within the household. Unfortunately, that may mean actually communicating with your family (I appreciate I am asking a lot) and working together. Things don't happen overnight and mistakes do happen but the more you communicate and the more you work together, the more you will achieve and you never know, you may actually realise that you like each other after all.

You need to establish a routine for your dog and stick to it, not just for this training programme but forevermore. You need to have set training times, set brain games, set playtimes and again this involves everyone not just Mam or Dad.

Start as you mean to go on. If you want the best for your dog and you want walks to be enjoyable again then you must implement these changes otherwise why have you wasted your time reading this book?

Putting the above into action does not need to take forever, but once the above is in place, you are now ready to move forward with your new training plan.

Start with the 'look at me' cue, practising at home to begin with, and over time (let me stress that word TIME) you can look at increasing the level of distraction to a point where you actually go out and look for another dog.

This process can be achieved in 1 week, 4 weeks sometimes even 1 year. We are all different, and we all learn at different paces; dogs are exactly the same so do not rush your dog and do not force him into a position where he feels uncomfortable or feels the need to have to react.

If you take your TIME (there is that word again), you are already on the road to success. Teaching your dog not to be afraid might take time, as it involves emotions. It may be the most time-consuming training that you have to do, but it is safe and sure. The best results are achieved if you do it carefully, step by step and focus on one thing at a time.

Understand that it is natural for a dog to be afraid, just like it is for us (you should see me watching a horror movie). Dog's cannot help it, and they are not reacting this way on purpose. It is up to us and your responsibility as a dog owner to help your dog overcome it.

If you follow the step by step guide and build up a reliable 'look at me' command, it won't be long before you are able to walk past another dog without any issues.

We know life can throw spanners in the work sometimes, and that is why we need to have back up plans, and that is why we have the U-turn and the sit and stay. These are designed to help get our dogs out of tricky situations, and although the 'look at me' command is the most important lesson to teach your dog, I do not want you to forget about these important aspects as if the unexpected were to happen and you were not prepared there is a good chance your hard work will go down the drain (we have all heard the expression of pissing in the wind right?)

Now, although I am sure you are a very responsible owner, there are always going to be others that we will class as 'those owners', you know which ones I mean. Those owners are the owners that do not respect other dog owners and allow their dog to do whatever it wants.

You need to continue focusing on your dog and ensuring that he is happy during his time with us. You need to appreciate and be prepared for the fact that your dog may never want to interact with another dog and that is not our aim, our aim is to get your dog comfortable enough to walk past another dog without any dramas.

Do not get me wrong by following this guide you will be able to desensitise your dog and recondition the unwanted behaviours, but some dogs are just not dog dogs, and some dogs prefer the company of their human companions.

So how can we make walks fun when our dog doesn't want to interact with other dogs? SIMPLE, make every walk an adventure walk!

This is something I do with my dog on every walk and something we do with our daycare dogs. Wherever we go, we have an adventure, and we make use of the natural environment. For example, I often get Buddy jumping over falling down logs, weaving in and out of bollards, crawling underneath benches, balancing on walls, 1-1 training and scent work. It helps keep walks fun for Buddy and me.

By making your walks into an adventure walk, you are not only physically exercising your dog, but you are mentally exercising your dog too, which helps keep your dog calm, focused and ultimately happy. Dogs are pleasers and love to work for things and they love attention from their owners. You may be thinking what is the point in that? I will just throw a ball for him that keeps him happy and although you may be right to a degree, dogs need variety and dogs need enrichment.

Not so long ago, I was out walking my dog, and I saw a guy sat in the boot of his car that was backed onto a field literally throwing a ball for his dog. The dog would fetch the ball and bring it back and then the process would be repeated. This is a cheaters way of tiring out your dog and not a very effective one. This dog was not receiving any form of mental stimulation or enrichment and in my honest opinion, I thought to myself, why even bother having a dog?

Keeping your dog focused on you prevents 'those owners' and their dogs from being a big distraction, and it makes walks fun and gives your dog what he needs.

As with us sometimes we can take two steps forward and then feel we are taking four steps back and this may happen from time to time with your dog during his training however do not be afraid to start again, remember the old saying 'Rome was not built in one day'…I don't actually know how long it took to build, but it certainly wasn't one day, and it certainly won't take one day to train your dog… trust me on that one.

Remember when following this guide to have fun, and no matter what, do not give up. You have it in you to do it; you just need to believe that you can and you will.

I do feel as the book has come to an end that now is the time to say this for one final time. To get the results you want, you must take your time, be patient and be consistent.

Bonuses

I hope you enjoyed reading the book, and I hope it has left you feeling motivated and ready to tackle this issue. Just remember that this book is only valuable if you take action.

I do appreciate that there is only so much you can take away from a book, so my first gift to you is **three short videos** to demonstrate the three training commands you have learnt from this book.

My second gift is a **checklist** for what you need in preparation for your dog's walk.

My third gift is a copy of our **training guide** to help with your dog's daily training.

To access these videos, checklist and training guide, please visit https://pets2impress.com/redeem-course/ and upon checkout enter the redemption code BOOKEXTRAS2019

About the Author

Tim Jackson started his career working with animals as a veterinary auxiliary nurse. He trained and qualified as a veterinary nurse in 2007 at Myerscough College. He was promoted to Head veterinary nurse and spent a number of years helping animals and their owners.

In 2008, Tim launched Pets2impress, a company that took the region by storm. What began as a pet sitting service soon expanded to offer a variety of services.

In 2013, Tim took the decision to leave his position as Head Veterinary nurse to expand Pets2impress.

Tim has completed multiple animal behaviour courses, including the Think Dog Certificates and a Diploma in Animal Behaviour. He passed each of these with a distinction and the knowledge he gained from these, combined with his extensive nursing experience, allowed him to offer one-on-one training sessions for all problem behaviours utilising only positive, reward-based training programmes.

This is a fun and stress-free method of training, which is easy to learn and rapidly achieves fantastic results. In its most basic form, it is a method of communication that is very clear for the dog. Examples of problem behaviours which Tim is able to assist with include separation anxiety, lack of basic training, dog-on-dog aggression and other anxiety-related issues, however, no problem is too small or too big for Tim.

In 2015 Tim opened a state of the art daycare facility, offering a safe and stimulating environment for dogs whilst their owners' are out at work. His experience as a qualified veterinary nurse, dog trainer and canine behaviourist gave him a comprehensive understanding that all dogs have different physical and emotional needs, allowing daycare sessions to be tailor-made to suit each individual.

Tim runs his daycare as close to a nursery setting as possible and therefore follows a daily schedule as closely as possible. This is extremely beneficial to the dogs in his care as it has been well documented that dogs thrive off predictability, and it has positive effects on both their behaviour and mental well being.

A typical day at the daycare centre includes free play, walks outside for a change of scenery, training time, and quiet time as rest is extremely important to prevent overstimulation, which can have a negative impact on both behaviour and physical condition. In October 2019 Tim launched an additional package to the daycare service, the doggy 'adventure' daycare to offer dog's further opportunity to receive physical and mental stimulation on a 1-1 basis as well as receive the other benefits daycare has to offer.

Tim is well known for his sense of humour and love and dedication to the welfare of all animals. Tim has owned several animals over the years including a rescue tarantula (which he was absolutely terrified of), an iguana, bearded dragons, cats, hamsters, rats, mice, fish and dogs.

Tim's mission in life is to help owners who struggle with their dog to prevent dogs ending up in shelter.

When not working Tim can be seen swapping Doggy daycare for Daddy daycare. Tim loves nothing more than spending time with his three adorable children. He can also be found out walking his dog Buddy and every now and then enjoys a nice pint at the local pub.

To find out more about Tim and Pets2impress, please visit the Pets2impress website www.pets2impress.com

Acknowledgements

As this is my first book, there are so many people I would like to thank, so many people that have supported me over the years and pushed me to always try harder. If I have forgotten anyone, oops… I'll try harder in my next book.

To the staff at Pets2impress 1. For putting up with me all of these years and laughing at my not so funny jokes and 2. For your support, enthusiasm and shared love you have for the dogs in our care. I couldn't do the job I do without my amazing team.

To my mentor Dominic Hodgson for giving me the push I needed to write my first (not my last) book.

To my good friend Katie Gee from Dogwood Adventure Play for recommending me to Dominic Hodgson and for your support over the years. Working together at Dogs Trust, she tolerated a lot of shit from me as we travelled around the country.

To my good friend Lauren Balmain Davies for giving me her honest criticism of this book and her dedicated support.

To my good friend Shannon Nixon for listening to my endless ideas and putting up with me on a daily basis.

To my Pets2impress clients that have been loyal to Pets2impress all these years. I would not be where I am today without your support, recommendations and dedication.

To my wonderful pets that I have had over the years that have taught me so much and given me so much love.

To the veterinary staff that I used to work with for their support and recommendations over the years.

And to my family and friends who are always there when I need them. I wouldn't be the person I am today without you. Special thanks to my wife, Rebecca, and my three adorable children, Sienna, Harvey and Darcey.

My final thanks must go to you. Thank you for choosing this book and spending the time to read it. I hope you found it useful and I hope you start to action the points made in this book. My mission is to try and prevent as many dogs ending up in shelter as possible, and if this book helps others, then I can sleep well at night. I ask if you found this book useful that you leave a review on Amazon… I will accept no less than a 5-star rating.

Tim Jackson, RVNBCCSDip.Fda

Printed in Great Britain
by Amazon

74756858R00043